# SOS
# Safely Obtaining Sobriety:
# The Alcohol Recovery Aid

George Legacy

*Copyright © 2010 Robert George Reoch Publishing*

*All rights reserved. No parts of this book may be used or reproduced by any means, graphic, electronic, or mechanical, including photocopying, recording, taping or by any information storage retrieval system without the written permission of the publisher except in the case of brief quotations embodied in critical articles and reviews.*

*This is a work of non-fiction. However, some of the characters, names, incidents, organizations, and dialogue in this novel are either the products of the author's imagination or are used fictitiously.*

*George Legacy*

*Visit: www.SOSSafelyObtainingSobriety.com*

*Because of the dynamic nature of the Internet, any Web addresses or links contained in this book may have changed since publication and may no longer be valid.*

*ISBN: 978-0-5780-7356-9 (ebook)*

*Other books from Robert George Reoch Publishing:*

Travelers' Shorts: *Stories That Move*

Travelers' Shorts 2: *Tethers*

*Visit: www.TravelersShorts.com*

# SOS Safely Obtaining Sobriety: The Alcohol Recovery Aid

## Introduction:

*Read this short introduction to know why you need this book.*

The goal is to get sober. To some people, just the physical act of obtaining sobriety—*trying to fight through withdrawal*—is the hardest step toward a larger goal of attaining long-term sobriety. You have to get sober first! This book will help the heavy drinker who has a desperate need to get sober now. It will also help anyone who is considering a long-term recovery from alcohol addiction. This is not a book about judging your character. It's about helping you to get started stopping, which can be the most difficult part. This book will tell you exactly what to do, and how to do it.

I know what it is like trying to stop. I was addicted to alcohol for over 20 years. I tried to stop drinking hundreds of times. There were dozens of Friday nights, when I would come home from work and immediately have a cocktail—even though I had promised myself I was going to dry-out over the weekend. I just couldn't do it. My mind and my body would not let me. I continued drinking heavily for years because I could not find the secret to quitting. Through trial and error, I finally discovered exactly how to get sober and stay sober. This book is for those who are in a struggle just to quit. This book is about safely obtaining sobriety—*getting sober without dying trying.* Read on. . . .

"Stop drinking before you kill yourself!"

Has that thought ever gone through your mind?

I had been near death three times due to my alcohol abuse, and I was at the point where I needed to do something about it quickly. I urgently needed to stop the insanity. I had already been through a 30-day rehabilitation program. I had attended numerous Alcoholics Anonymous meetings. I had even tried mathematically calculating how to decrease my alcohol consumption, thinking I could stop drinking gradually, on my own. All of my efforts, including rehab, seemed only to make things worse for me. Throughout most of my adult life, it was as though I were slowly drowning.

*I needed a life preserver.*

Have you reached the point where you think you could be killing yourself? Do you find yourself unable to stop drinking? Do you get sick when you try? Perhaps you make it for a day or two without alcohol, but then you can't get past that third day without at least one drink. Then, that one drink turns into two, then three, and then you're gone. You find you must drink to survive—but you want to stop.

In this book, I can tell you how to save yourself from being underwater, so to speak. I can show you how to emerge alive and kicking, *safely.* Getting sober isn't that complicated, however when you have reached the point where you can't stop, it is not safe to stop drinking all at once. My plan is quite simple. I can even say it is easy to execute. You can make my plan y*our* plan. It worked for me. You can get sober and survive it.

I believe my book is the most useful alcohol recovery book you will ever read because it tells you exactly what to do. It tells you how to get started safely and how to put this information to good use immediately. I have written this book to help. If you follow my simple plan and make it yours, you will get your life back under your own control, not under alcohol's control.

Think of this book as your life preserver. That's what you need when you're drowning. Whether you're in an ocean of salt water, or in a sea of booze, you need someone to throw you a life ring and it doesn't matter if it comes from a total stranger.

I am tossing that life ring to you now. Grab onto it quickly and stop sinking further into alcoholic disaster.

# Contents

Introduction

Chapter 1: My story

Chapter 2: Are These Your Symptoms?

Chapter 3: What To Do — Setting Your Mind to It

Chapter 4: The New Tool

Chapter 5: This is Remarkable!

Chapter 6: My Plan — Your Plan

Chapter 7: Remind Yourself of Pending Disaster

Chapter 8: Conclusion

## Chapter 1: My Story

Was I was born with a propensity for alcohol addiction? My grandfather was an alcoholic, and my mother had problems with prescription drugs and alcohol, but that's as far as I've gone with any question concerning heredity. It's enough to know that I'm an alcoholic. I don't have any children, nor am I planning to have any, therefore I won't be passing along any traits.

My first taste of alcohol came when I was eleven years old. A pal asked me if I wanted to drink some tequila. There was a bottle in his father's liquor cabinet. My friend poured some of the booze into a small mouthwash bottle and we took it with us while we went carousing around our neighborhood one night. It took only a few sips of tequila before I was drunk. I wound up punching my friend in the mouth, thinking it was funny and not realizing the impact—not knowing that I had actually hurt him. My buddy stopped hanging out with me after that. It was not until years later that I recalled what had happened and then realized why I had lost that friend. Children should not drink alcohol. It took me quite some time to put that early experience into perspective.

Raised by a single divorced mother, I rarely saw her drink, but there was usually a bottle of wine in the refrigerator, the kind with the screw-on cap. I began taking occasional small sips from the bottle. I enjoyed the little buzz it gave me and nobody ever seemed to notice. Sometimes, I would drink more than just a few sips. Afraid of being caught, I would replace some of the wine by pouring a small amount of water into the bottle. I always got away with it.

When I was in junior high school, we moved to a new town and I made some new friends. The older I got, the wider became my range of friends, and the more access I had to booze. A few of the older teens would share alcohol with the younger ones. Once, at a cast party after the high school play, I shared a pint of Southern Comfort with one of my friends in order to impress some girls. My friend later had to help me, as I staggered home on foot. I threw up several times on the way home and woke up in the back seat of my mother's parked car, wondering where my pants and shoes were. It was my first alcohol blackout.

Another time, after a Halloween party in high school, I went joy riding in an older teen's car and several friends. We toilet papered houses while passing around a bottle of bourbon. Later that night, one of my friends and I were dropped off at the high school parking lot. As I lay passed-out on the asphalt, a stranger came by and admonished my friend to get me some help. I remember hearing an older adult saying something about my being in bad shape, suggesting that I needed some liquid or coffee. One of my older siblings was summoned to pick me up and I was brought home to sleep it off. I had my first truly debilitating hangover the next day and stayed home from school.

One summer, my mother had her four youngest children taken away, including me. After a long downward spiral, Mom had had a mental breakdown and was admitted to a rehabilitation facility. Her substance abuse (alcohol, marijuana, and pills) had left her unstable. We younger ones all were sent to separate foster homes.

While in foster care, I thrived in a new home with responsible parents who were also loving and nurturing. I still had wide exposure to alcohol and marijuana through my friends at school and among my three adult siblings, who were then living on their own. However, I was too busy with extracurricular school activities to allow drugs or alcohol to interfere with my life. I was active in band, sports, speech, and other positive outlets, all of which consumed most of my free time outside of the classroom. I was having too much fun to get into trouble.

As I transitioned from high school to junior college, I took on full-time jobs in a variety of fields, from factory worker to taxi driver. By age twenty, I was drinking modestly to the point of mainly drinking a few beers on weekends and generally not getting into any serious trouble. When I reached age twenty-one, I discovered bars and cocktails. My favorite drink became a gin and tonic. In the disco age, it also became my habit to frequent nightclubs and to drink and dance until the bars closed. Those early adult years evolved into a long stream of one-night stands and brief relationships—a perfectly normal life for a young man with no attachments at that age.

I eventually found a solid opportunity in the telecommunications field and began a long stable career. By my mid-twenties, I was settled in my job. I had a decent apartment and a nice car. Meanwhile, my lifestyle outside of work had changed very little. I continued to frequent bars until all hours of the night. I had no interest in getting married or settling down. I managed to perform well at work, although I was often coming in late or calling in sick and getting away with it. I was physically fit, so I was able to sustain that lifestyle, without serious consequences, for years.

One New Year's Eve, after drinking heavily at a local bar, I asked a friend to drive me home in my car, not realizing that he, too, was drunk. In a dense fog, he became lost and drove us off a cliff. The car tumbled several hundred feet down the side of a mountain and into a ravine. We both survived, battered, but without any catastrophic injuries. However, my car was demolished. Unfortunately, I was found in the driver's seat of my overturned car, and the police assumed I had been driving. I was charged with the misdemeanor crime of Driving Under the Influence (DUI). Unfortunately, my former friend dodged all responsibility for the accident and I was stuck with the consequences. I had to pay a large fine for the DUI and pay the costs to repair damages to a city fence. My driver's license was restricted for a year and my driving record was ruined. I was financially impacted for several years because of the jump in my auto insurance rates. As if that were all not a heavy enough blow, I also needed to buy another car.

     A few years later, after another late night out at the clubs, while driving home I was pulled over by the police for having a non-working taillight. With alcohol on my breath, I was given a sobriety test, failed, and was arrested again for a DUI. This would be my second DUI as far as the courts were concerned, even though I knew I had been wrongly convicted of the first. A second DUI meant an even larger fine than the first. I spent thousands of dollars on the best lawyer I could find and he was able to have my second DUI treated as a first offense. The resulting costs were astronomical. I had just purchased a new sports car, so my insurance rates took another drastic leap higher. For what I was paying in auto insurance premiums, I could have been buying a new home. Instead, drinking and cars kept me out of the housing market for years.

     Alcohol abuse causes temporary insanity, which can also lead to other bad habits. The 1980s were a time of experimentation on several levels for me. Friends came offering various powdered substances as well as marijuana and other drugs on an almost daily basis. Only my guardian angels know how I managed to avoid utter self-destruction. There were parties in Beverly Hills with cocaine in piles on top of mirrored glass cocktail tables. There was snorting in backrooms of flashy clubs in Palm Springs. I sometimes went entire weekends with little or no sleep. At work, half of my coworkers were addicted to "crystal" (crystal methamphetamine). Absenteeism was common. I always believed I was immune to addiction because I felt as though I knew when to stop. In fact, the odd thing was that I never once paid for drugs and I never kept them in my home. I made it a point never to buy. I was happy just to drink and get drunk, although I rarely turned down a line offered to me by friends here and there. Drugs were nearly impossible to avoid and even harder to refuse while drinking.

What actually saved me from becoming completely engulfed in the drug scene was my personal fanaticism about exercise and going to the gym. I had become somewhat of a poster boy for the '80s fitness craze. I rarely missed a daily session at the gym no matter what I had been doing the night before. I would jump around for hours in group aerobics, swim laps in the pool, lift weights, or run on the beach listening to "Chariots of Fire" on my walkman. That regimen likely saved me from becoming an out-of-shape, full-time drug user.

Despite my extravagances outside of work, I was relatively ambitious and successful in my career. Considering my frequent drinking, I would likely have been deemed a high-functioning alcoholic at the time. I was able to stay healthy enough, and in such control that I could still pursue advancement at my company. Part of the criteria in considering a promotion involved assessing my standing in the community. In order to demonstrate social responsibility and involvement, I undertook to coach a boys' soccer team during off-hours after work. I made time for conducting soccer practices during weeknights as well as for coaching games on weekends. I had played soccer in school. I had also frequently played backyard sports with my young nephews, so this challenge came easier than I had expected.

I ran simple skill-building drills with my young soccer team of six and seven-year-olds. I followed the model of making sure that every kid played and that everyone had fun. I began every practice by having the kids play a warm-up game of duck-duck goose to loosen up, and then followed that by teaching them the basics of moving and passing a soccer ball. One night per week was a change from my usual routine of going to the gym directly after work, but it did not alter my regular habit of going out drinking later.

In my soccer coaching strategy, I applied what I refer to as my "Vince Lombardi Method" of soccer coaching. I would hold up a soccer ball in one hand and say to my young players, "This is a soccer ball." Then, pointing to a soccer net at one end of the field, I would add with emphasis, "That is the goal ... Your job is to get the soccer ball into the goal." It was as simple as that. I would encourage my team, during each game, to keep moving the ball in the direction of the goal, using all their passing and kicking skills to get the ball into the net. We won every one of our games and placed first in our division. Nobody got hurt, everyone played, and we all had fun. I still recall our awards luncheon at a local Pizza Hut at the end of the season. I was proud, but actually felt bored and anxious. All I wanted to do was to go home and drink.

Eventually, I was promoted at work. In my new position, I became successful as a training instructor. It was also around that time that I began to notice my relationship with alcohol was becoming a strain. The effects of heavy drinking had begun to affect my judgment and my confidence in responding appropriately to certain challenges. As an instructor, I sometimes had to deal with difficult adult students. There were times when it was all I could do to keep from having a meltdown when an adult student behaved like a child. I was concerned that I might one day react inappropriately and thus jeopardize my career.

As years passed, my drinking became more frequent. I never drank while at work, except on rare occasions when a business luncheon toast was in order. However, when my job responsibilities frequently came to involve extensive traveling, including weeklong stays in distant cities, my drinking became even more excessive. Bored and alone, I would buy a bottle of vodka to keep in my hotel room. I would sometimes drink half of a quart bottle in one night, in addition to a few cocktails with dinner at the hotel bar. It became a regular habit while away on business.

The first time I went into an alcohol rehabilitation program was when I woke up at home one Sunday morning and realized I had drunk an entire quart of vodka the night before, all alone. For months, I had been noticing my drinking getting heavier. I had become aware that although my desire was to cut down, I had actually been drinking more than ever. I had even developed a morbid fascination about how much alcohol I could put away in a single night. I wondered if I could ever get as bad as to drink and entire bottle of vodka in one night.

When I woke up one morning and realized I had done just that, I knew then, I had gone too far. I needed to get help.

I called my closest friend and we discussed my situation. I decided to admit myself to a rehabilitation program before it was too late, before I became seriously ill. After making the decision, and without hesitating, I packed a few things to take with me to the hospital. When my friend picked me up, we went out to breakfast and I drank a last Bloody Mary for a laughs. Then, my friend drove me to the rehabilitation facility, which I had chosen from a list provided by my company health plan. I had quietly been looking into the rehab option in the months prior, so I already knew I had an escape hatch, although I had only a remote intention of going and a vague idea of what to expect. My friend parked in front of the two-story facility. It appeared it was formerly a large tract home. It had little else but a sign in front to distinguish it from the other tract homes in the neighborhood, which was located just off a major freeway.

At the check-in desk, the admitting person allowed me to call my boss to let him know of my decision. My boss was kind and supportive, and assured me that I need not worry about anything except my immediate concern. It was a brief, but encouraging conversation. Following that call, I said goodbye to my friend and turned to face the music in the clinic.

The first thing they did was to give me drugs–a few pills–which were meant to help buffer the effects of withdrawal and to help me to avoid possible seizures. They also administered sedatives to help me sleep for the first 24 hours or so. I was awakened at intervals for additional doses of medications, and then allowed to return to bed. The first few days in the facility involved mostly sleep while my body withdrew from alcohol.

The thirty days I spent in rehab are now just odd memories. The members of the staff all had vastly different personalities. My fellow patients were a widely diverse group too. There was a young, twenty-something boy, fresh off the streets, a part-time porn actor, who had come in to the facility to get off crystal meth. There was an elderly woman who had been drinking two quarts of vodka a day and finally agreed to treatment after spewing vodka laced Kool-Aid into the face of her neighbor who had come to check on her well-being. There was an attractive lesbian with the look of a rock star. She was terminally perky to the point of being annoying. The others in the group were either boring or scary, or both. I don't recall their faces.

Treatment in rehab consisted of a month's stay with alternating daily routines. Everyone participated in lengthy group sessions on a daily basis. We listened to long, sometimes useful, factual lectures about alcohol's effects. Some lectures were about how alcohol makes us completely powerless over our lives. Many discussions focused on the effects that alcohol abusers have on other peoples' lives. We ate breakfast, lunch, and dinner from a buffet served in a large dining area that was once the garage of the spacious home. We were taken on field trips to attend Alcoholics Anonymous (AA) meetings and Narcotics Anonymous (NA) meetings in various surrounding communities. Most of the gatherings were held in meeting rooms at churches. As part of our therapy, we also visited nearby parks where we played croquet for the sake of social interaction, exercise, and fresh air. In the evenings, larger group gatherings were held, in which family and friends attended for support. Those experiences were often awkward and emotional for most of the families. My best friend and my younger sister came.

The most significant personal change that I took away from thirty days in rehab was a profound sense that I was somehow a failure. AA meetings were excruciating exercises in self-pity and regret. Meetings involved one person at a time volunteering to stand up and tell a personal story about something related to alcoholism and how it had affected their lives—or they could simply ramble about anything they were feeling at the time, as long as it was not too heated or overtly hostile. It was all strictly voluntary.

Most of what took place at AA meetings merely brought me down. As a firm believer in the power of positive thinking, I found most of what went on in those meetings to be counterproductive. In my own personal development, I had already discovered numerous philosophies and ways of thinking that were completely at odds with much of what I heard in Alcoholics Anonymous meetings. I had long before learned to think positively in the face of diversity and to move forward, and not look back on, or dwell on, negative experiences. I could find no useful purpose in convincing people to declare openly that they were powerless and that alcohol or drugs had "won." It was as though resigning oneself to being a second-class citizen for the rest of one's life.

Alcoholics Anonymous encourages participation in a twelve-step program, which aspires to make you own-up to your mistakes and to make amends to others you have hurt. My problem with that is that not every alcoholic has left a wake of destruction in his or her lives. Some alcoholics are perfectly successful people whose drinking has become an addiction. Everyone makes mistakes in their lives. Some alcoholics make fewer mistakes than non-alcoholics do. To try to convince the alcoholic that he or she has made the one big, end-all mistake of their lives is nonsense. What is the point of going back and deconstructing one's life in twelve steps? How does that help? If there are unresolved issues, those certainly can be addressed without a daunting program of searching for fault and asking for forgiveness, and putting it all under the heading of alcoholism. To my mind, that only magnifies the problem and does little to help a person move ahead. I believe the individual needs to choose carefully his or her path in handling recovery. It does not need to make one feel repentant for the rest of their lives.

After I completed my thirty-day rehabilitation program and attended a few follow-up group meetings, I was alcohol free for nearly 60 days. I then returned to drinking. I drank lightly at first. I chose to drink again mainly because I felt I could keep it under control and because my social circle was comprised almost entirely of friends and family who all drank frequently. After rehab, I felt better equipped to watch out for warning signs of excessive drinking. I decided I would be able to manage my own situation within the same social confines in which I had spent the past few decades and somehow avoid drinking to excess. I felt as though I was succeeding and had gained control over my life again. I bought myself a new sports car. Things went fine for several months.

At work, I began to experience a common pitfall in the corporate management world. As I advanced in positions from being a training instructor to a more dynamic position as a training designer, I soon discovered that my new boss was from a different planet. She often seemed distracted and out of touch, making arbitrary decisions and giving nonsensical direction that ran counter to my basic sensibilities. My biggest fear was that I might become just like her, my worst idea of a corporate manager, and then end up being fired for being stupid. At my new manager's discretion, I often was sent to distant cities to attend meetings that had nothing to do with my position. Expectations of me became so undefined that I usually had no idea where to place focus. I was a capable and talented manager and I was being underutilized. My manager switched directions on a weekly basis. It became such that I was never expected to finish anything I had started. I was never at a point of not meeting expectations because projects were continuously being changed due to needs of the business. My position at work was frustrating, to put it plainly.

I was at the height of my career and financial success, yet I found myself spending half of my workday either participating in unnecessary conference calls or spending my time at the gym just to pass the hours. I remained electronically tethered to my job via cell phone and pager, so I could go to my office whenever I liked. I could even telecommute from home and do absolutely nothing, and still receive my comfortable salary. In my odd state of professional limbo, it became easier for me to drink at the end of the day.

I had a safe haven at home. Fortunately, during my career, I had saved enough money to purchase a beautiful condominium. I lived in a 24-hour community on the cutting edge of modern urban planning. I enjoyed an Olympic sized pool and a gym. I was in walking distance of bars and restaurants. There were grocery stores and video rental shops just steps away—I had everything. I could also drink as much as I wanted while staying out of trouble. I didn't need to drive anywhere. Even my best friend lived just a few blocks away.

Around this time, my friend learned he had AIDS. It was an unexpected shock. With all of my wild flings in the '80s, I had escaped that danger by practicing safe sex. My best friend since junior high school was not so lucky. He was not especially promiscuous. It was believed he contracted HIV from a needle, possibly during a visit to the doctor. In the years that followed his diagnosis, I spent as much time with my friend as I could. With his apartment in close proximity to mine, I visited frequently. We spent hours sitting at his kitchen table drinking and playing cards. He never gave up his vices such as drinking and smoking. He took his medications, followed most of his doctor's advice, and still lived as rich a life as possible despite some up-and-down struggles. During many nights of shared laughter and tears, alcohol buffered the pain and buoyed our spirits as our friendship endured my friend's battle.

I had always believed physical addiction applied only to drugs such as heroin and cocaine. I had thought alcoholics were more akin to bums and hobos than to victims of chemical dependency. I never dreamed I could actually develop a physical addiction to alcohol until it was too late. In the years spent with my friend, I tried to be as lively as possible, which for me had always meant drinking to elevation. I had been rather shy as child, except when performing in a play or singing in the choir. As I grew older and became a more self-conscious teen, alcohol became the crutch that allowed me to become the star of the senior play, or to win the speech tournament. Later, booze made me the best dancer in the clubs and the most interesting conversationalist at parties. Alcohol also allowed me to reminisce with my friend on those many nights of playing cards or backgammon long into the early hours of the morning. All along, my brain was becoming chemically altered to expect alcohol on a regular basis. Without realizing it, I was becoming physically addicted to alcohol.

I sometimes drank while exploring on the internet. I was part of a new phenomenon of people meeting other people online. I eventually met someone special online and wound up involved in a permanent relationship. While dating, my drinking continued as always. I never tried to hide the fact that I enjoyed drinking. Over time, the relationship became established and committed. My life had taken another turn.

About six months into my new relationship, I received sudden news that my best friend had passed on. He died unexpectedly on Christmas day as he sat napping in a chair at a family member's home. I received a call from his sister the following day, gently breaking the news. I was devastated. It was the greatest pain I had ever experienced, even though I had known it was coming. My friend could barely walk more than a block in the last years of his life because of difficulty in breathing. He had never stopped smoking. He was addicted to nicotine. I believe smoking is what contributed most to his death, not AIDS. Zachary was loved by many people. He left a lasting impression on all of us who knew him.

I moved to New England. My new life partner was offered a promising position in Boston and I was ready to follow and make a change. Coincidently, my company had been offering early retirement around that same time, so I volunteered to resign. I accepted a generous parting package and left the company as soon as I was able. I knew it was the right time for me to get off the corporate track. I was destined for other things. I found the courage to do what others only dreamed of doing by quitting my job. I leased out my condominium and moved with my partner to Boston.

We rented an apartment in Malden, Massachusetts, which is a large suburb north of Boston. An acquaintance had recommended Malden because of its central location and affordability. Our new flat was on the eighth floor of a high-rise building with a great view of the Boston skyline in the distance. We were close to a major grocery store and there were a few small restaurants in the neighborhood. Living in Malden, however, turned out to be less than an ideal situation for me.

While my other half worked, I spent most of my time at home by myself. There was nothing to do outdoors in Malden. There were no nearby trails for running or bicycling. The streets were congested and tangled, making walking anywhere unpleasant. Our apartment building was inhabited mainly by large immigrant families with whom we had nothing in common, thus we had no immediate social interaction. Our ten-story apartment building, with its hundreds of units, had only two elevators. Both of the elevators were slow, and worse, usually one of the two lifts was out of service, making getting in and out of the building frustrating and troublesome. I spent three years feeling fairly isolated in the apartment, although my relationship with my partner remained strong and happy. I was glad to be off the corporate track. I was enjoying a break from decades of working for the same company, yet, as they say, idle hands are tools of the devil.

During our time in Malden, I drank and watched hundreds of rented movies to pass the time. I also honed my cooking skills, preparing lavish meals on a daily basis.

When I wasn't watching movies or cooking, I spent time writing and illustrating a children's book (which I never had published). I also tried to visit regularly a nearby YMCA gym that was in an old brick building, which was dank and not very well equipped. My workouts became less frequent as winters set in and it became difficult to get to the gym in the snow. I began to gain weight. Over time, my main interest became drinking. After the first two years in Malden, my drinking eventually reached a level that required me to drink just to function.

My partner and I enjoyed traveling several times a year. I always looked forward to getting away, although my drinking sometimes made travel a precarious undertaking. We toured, by car, throughout New England. We also took trips to various cities by plane, spending weeks in Miami, Washington D.C., and Philadelphia, to mention a few. We especially enjoyed taking the train to New York City, if just for a weekend. On our trips, I often brought along small bottles of vodka to keep handy in our hotel rooms. I needed the booze to fortify myself before going out and seeing the sights. The vodka had less of an odor, but I also carried breath mints wherever I went.

My drinking eventually reached the point where I found myself frequently feeling dizzy. I would often stay up late into the early hours of the morning, drinking and writing. I would ultimately go to bed and blackout, rising again around noon, or sometimes even later. Waking up late in the day gave me just a few hours to shower, go to the grocery store, and then return home to prepare dinner. I always needed to buy more alcohol while shopping.

As I showered before going out, I often worried about falling down in the tub. I could feel myself fading in and out of consciousness as I washed my hair. I even came to be afraid of closing my eyes in the shower. I never spoke of this to anyone. It sounded too awful to admit. As I continued drinking more heavily, I even began hiding little bottles of vodka around the apartment. I needed to keep saturated in alcohol in order to function. I slowly came to realize that I had a physical addiction.

When I had my first seizure, I never knew what hit me. I became semi-aware that I was in the hospital only after sleeping for a few days, but I was still barely aware of my surroundings as I faded in and out. There was a feeding tube in my stomach and a catheter in my penis. I continued to sleep for three more days while my body detoxified and my risk of seizure diminished. My partner came and went, frequently checking on my condition. He had witnessed my seizure and had called the paramedics to our apartment.

We had been watching Sunday football on television when it happened. As I was sitting on the couch, my eyes rolled back in my head and I went into convulsions. My body stiffened in seizures of rigidity and shaking. I peed myself and lost consciousness. Worse, I stopped breathing. Fortunately, because of the rapid response of the fire department, trained emergency medical technicians arrived in time to save my life. I vaguely recall being briefly awake as I was wheeled on a gurney down the hall of our apartment building.

My hospitalization was like being in heaven. I had only to sleep soundly and occasionally dream. I remember finally getting out of bed and using the bathroom before being checked-out and then going home. It had been nearly a week. That was my first seizure.

I had never expected anything like that to happen to me. I had been trying to cut down my alcohol consumption because of my fears of falling in the shower or worse. On the day we were watching football, I had drunk very little since the night before. It had been several hours since my body had ingested any alcohol. My brain rebelled with an electrical malfunction and I had a gran mal seizure.

In the weeks after my hospitalization, typical of my personality, I chose not to take my seizure too seriously. It was an anomaly as far as I was concerned. I had hardly ever gotten sick. It could not possibly happen again. After about a month, I even concluded that since I had dried out, I could begin drinking again. I told myself I would simply keep it under control.

On the contrary, that's not how it works with addiction. My brain had already been altered from decades of heavy drinking. Once an alcoholic's brain has been conditioned for high levels of alcohol, it develops a tolerance. The more an alcoholic drinks, the more alcohol it takes to reach that "click," that point where an alcoholic feels the high—the buzz. Over time, that set point in the brain becomes more difficult to reach, requiring the alcoholic to increase alcohol intake to achieve that *click*. As the brain chemistry is altered, the rules change for the alcoholic, often without the drinker even realizing it.

I must be clear: *I am not a medical expert in this process*. My understanding of physical changes brought on by alcohol abuse is based on years of personal experience as well as from informed lectures from experts in treating alcoholism. I have also read from numerous reliable sources on alcoholism and its effects on the brain. It is not my intent to educate on the finer points of the physiological processes of the brain. Rather, it is my goal to describe what I have learned and to offer a workable solution. You can escape your addiction safely, without seizures, but it requires careful planning to do it successfully. Once detoxified and sober, the long-term aspects of recovery require your own personal commitment.

I began drinking again barely a month after leaving the hospital. I promised myself I would drink only one or two drinks per day, maybe three. However, once a bottle was opened and I was drinking from it, the game was on again. Even after thirty days of sobriety, my brain remembered its set point. At first, I got by with a glass, or two, of wine in restaurants. Then, at home, I began drinking vodka again, or bourbon, or both, *and* wine. The holiday season had come around again and I could not resist partaking of my favorite holiday cocktails. My habits returned quickly. I subconsciously stood outside myself and watched as I gradually increased my drinking.

I managed to fly home to visit family and friends a few weeks before Christmas. I made my usual rounds, but also cancelled a few visits, instead staying in my hotel, drinking. I hadn't wanted to sleep at the homes of family or friends because I knew I wouldn't be able to drink in the manner to which I was accustomed. I would look like a monster if I were to be seen swilling vodka all day. On the other hand, I had to drive my rented car to see family without drinking and driving. Some visits went very well. Some were chores. There are people in my family that I can barely tolerate. It was a delicate balancing act trying to maintain equilibrium. I was glad when it came time to fly home.

It was a long flight back to Boston. I drank on the plane, the same as I had done on the flight out. I knew that I had to do it. I had a sick feeling that if I did not have several drinks, something bad would happen to me.

Once back in Boston, I began doing more research on alcoholism. I discovered new things about my condition that I had not known before, such as alcohol's long-term effects on brain chemistry. I learned that the brain goes haywire once it has been exposed to long-term alcohol abuse. I acknowledged to myself that my brain was surely messed up and I wanted to find a way to fix it.

In the corporate world, I had served as a project manager on some major projects. I once was tasked with reconfiguring the largest California telephone company's handling of its incoming business calls, and then training all of its employees on how to handle the changes. It was a yearlong project requiring extensive planning and onsite work throughout the state. My skills in project management became finely honed during the process. I decided to put those skills to use by applying them to my own situation. I would devise a plan to free myself of my alcoholic nightmare.

While researching my new self-help project, I happened across information about a new drug called "Campral." (See Chapter 4 for more about this drug.) I learned that Campral could help alleviate my craving for alcohol once I was sober again. I realized that if I could get sober safely, I could move ahead using the new drug. After more research, I then devised a simple plan that I could follow to achieve my goal of obtaining sobriety again. My goal was to get sober safely, and to remain sober indefinitely. (Chapter 6 is the simple plan.)

Having made it through the holiday season alive, I was well aware that my physical dependence on alcohol needed to be addressed. I knew my plan to get sober involved undergoing a controlled detoxification while under close medical supervision in the hospital. In the meantime, in prior months, my partner had made plans for us to visit Montreal in the summer. We had also scheduled a few interim road trips in the New England area. I put off my plans to get sober until after our travels.

I could then give my full commitment to my project's success. On our trips, I brought along a few bottles of vodka, meting out the booze over the duration and drinking moderately at restaurants too. I managed to pace myself and enjoy most of our touring. I realized later that I would have been at great risk for having another seizure had I not continued drinking while we were away from home. I chose not to cancel any travel plans in deference to my partner. It was important that I do it for him and not allow my situation to deny him of well-deserved vacations. I also wanted to be entirely undistracted from my project, with no other plans in the works, once I got started.

Unfortunately, after our latest round of traveling was over, several events at home conspired to keep me from my plan to get sober again. There were minor doctor appointments for unrelated small health issues. I also needed to have some major dental work done, which added a series of scheduled appointments to my calendar. Before I knew it, the holiday season was upon us again. I decided to stay in Boston for Christmas as opposed to risking another long flight to California. I would fly out for another visit the following February. All the while, I still had my plan for getting sober in mind. I was determined to go forward as soon as all other distractions had been eliminated.

Shortly after Thanksgiving, I had another seizure. My partner described it as a mini seizure. As with my first, I have no recollection of it happening. While sitting on the sofa, watching television, I apparently blacked out and had a few minor convulsions. My partner was able to wake me up. I had been drinking only moderately, less than usual, and my body somehow had a bad reaction. I believe it was probably because I had curtailed my drinking too quickly that I had another seizure. We drove to the hospital and I was examined and then kept several hours for observation. When we later returned home, I immediately went to bed and slept. I awoke the next day having no recollection of events. It was not until months later that my partner explained what had happened.

I made it through the holidays again, but I was drinking heavily as usual. I was still planning to go ahead with my project to get sober. I even visited my doctor and requested a prescription for Campral. I was surprised that my doctor had not heard of the drug. It was *that new*, apparently. While I waited in the exam room, my doctor checked her resources and found the information she needed about Campral. She wrote me a prescription without hesitation. My project was starting out smoothly.

Then, in February, an urgent business situation required me to travel to California unexpectedly. Just as I was about to move ahead with my plan, an unexpected minor emergency required me to fly to San Diego for a weeklong stay. While in San Diego I had originally planned to stay at my sister's home, but she cancelled at the last minute and I spent much of the week getting drunk in my hotel room. I completed my business in San Diego and boarded a flight back to Boston.

I was about to have my third and most serious seizure upon returning to Boston. My flight from San Diego was long and miserable. On the plane, I was seated next to a very large, obese person whose girth spilled over to my seat. The flight was completely full, so I could not change seats. I had nowhere to rest my elbows during the log flight, so I kept my hands folded in my lap and got out of my seat only once to stretch. There were times during the flight when I felt I might have a panic attack, something, which I had never had happen before. I felt claustrophobic. I avoided drinking alcohol because I was afraid it would exasperate my cramped situation even more. That choice was a bad mistake. By the time we were nearing Boston, I was feeling faint and nauseous. As we approached the airport, I summoned a flight attendant and asked to be let off the plane first. I explained I was feeling extremely ill.

Thankfully, the flight attendant responded with urgency. I was provided the first exit from the plane as well as wheelchair service to the seating area at the gate. An ambulance was offered to me, but I knew my partner would be coming to pick me up, so I walked through the airport feeling dizzy and nauseous, retrieved my luggage from baggage claim, and then met my partner outdoors, at the curb, as planned. We drove home. I was still feeling ill.

Once at home, my condition worsened. I knew I needed a drink, so I made a quick cocktail of bourbon and cola, drank a few sips, and then lay down on the sofa. Within minutes, I felt I was going to vomit. I went to the bathroom and began throwing up violently a brownish liquid. Not realizing I had been vomiting blood, I said nothing about it to my partner. I went back to lie on the couch again. A few days later, I awoke in the hospital—again. Again, I had no recollection of having had another gran mal seizure. As I learned, it is typical for a person not to have memories of such events.

While in the hospital, I was examined by a gastroenterologist who discovered I had multiple bleeding stomach ulcers and a critical weakening in the vein connecting my esophagus to my liver. Even though my liver was healthy—a miracle in itself—the artery of concern was damaged from years of pressure caused by chronic backup of alcohol waiting to be processed by my liver. It is a condition known as esophageal varices, which can be caused heavy drinking and by cirrhosis of the liver. Apparently, the long flight home from San Diego, with my having sat cramped in my seat, had aggravated conditions in my stomach. I was told by the specialist that if the blood vessel had ruptured, or if it were to rupture in the future, it could cause a bleed-out and I could die. Just one more drink could cause a rupture, she said. I took her word. That final straw convinced me to stop drinking. After detoxifying in the hospital for a week, I went home and began taking Campral.

My life changed for the better after that last hospitalization, which was actually one of the steps in my plan (even though it did not wait for me to implement). Changes did not come all at once after I became sober again, but I have not had a drink since. Once I stopped drinking, my head needed a few months to defog completely. Although my brain chemistry had been altered by years of drinking, the prescription Campral enabled my brain to begin rewiring itself. I noticed some changes right away. (In Chapter 5, I discuss in more detail how my daily living changed while on Campral therapy.) To this day, as far as I can tell, my brain now behaves in the same way as it did before I became addicted to alcohol. I have had no cravings for over three years and I have experienced no side effects whatsoever. At this writing, I have been sober since March 9, 2007.

Since sobering up, I have traveled extensively. I have also begun a new career. With renewed clarity of mind, I have even published this book. I hope these pages help you and others who may be struggling with addiction. Understanding the importance of safely getting sober, you can follow my plan and use it to make your own strides. It is far too risky to try to quit an addiction on your own, without help. The consequences can be catastrophic (as I have learned from my own brushes with death). The best way to move on with your life is by first safely obtaining sobriety. Read on and this book will tell you how to do it.

    Best regards and good luck!

    George Legacy

# Chapter 2: Are These Your Symptoms?

You may have a physical addiction to alcohol if any of these conditions apply to you:

*Your face is usually flushed (pink or reddish).*

When you look in the mirror, is your face flushed pink or red? Does your appearance make you look as though you are wind burned or sun burned, even when you haven't been outdoors?

*You perspire readily.*

Do you sweat easily? Do you perspire simply getting dressed? Do you wear fewer clothes because you constantly feel warm and sticky? Does anxiety cause you to break out in a sweat? If you go too long without a drink, does your skin turn clammy and moist? Does mild exertion cause you to sweat profusely? Near the end of your workday at the office, does your body begin to sweat until you can leave and get a drink?

*You feel dizzy often.*

Do you feel you might lose your balance or fall when you close your eyes in the shower? Do you get dizzy and anxious in public? Do elevators make you feel nervous or panicky? Do you worry when driving that you may pass out at the wheel, even when you have not been drinking? While standing in a line at the grocery store, do you sometimes feel faint? Does tying your shoes make you dizzy? Do you have moments when your vision goes dim or the room suddenly seems to lurch?

*Your hands shake.*

Do your hands tremble when you hold them out flat? Do your hands shake when you prepare a drink? When you sign your name on a check or a document, does your signature appear different than it usually does? Do you rush signing a document when someone is watching?

*You feel anxious on airplanes.*

Does the thought of flying cause you anxiety? Does business flying bother you now, when it was never a problem before? Do you worry about how you will appear if you order a few drinks during a flight? Do you secretly want to order three or four cocktails—or more?

*You wake up feeling drained.*

When you rise in the morning, do you feel as though in a deep fog? Are you sluggish or anxious? Do you feel you function better after you have had a few drinks?

*You drink particularly excessively before going to bed.*

Do you drink extra before going to bed so that it will carry you through the first half of the following day? Do you need a high level of residual alcohol in your system to make it through your workday without a drink?

*You sometimes fear contact with other people.*

Do you try to find ways to cut short your interactions with others at work? Do you avoid speaking before groups you have spoken in front of in the past? Do you fear running into your boss in airports or hotels because you might say something inappropriate?

*You hide booze.*

Do you keep a stash of vodka somewhere at home that nobody else knows about? Do you sneak off to grab a quick shot from a hidden bottle when you are already drinking a glass of wine in another room? Do you keep hard liquor in your hotel room while away on business?

*An alcohol purchase is one of your first priorities in your daily schedule.*

Do you manage part of your day around your next alcohol purchase? Is buying alcohol frequently the foremost thing on your mind each day until you have made that purchase?

*You mete out your alcohol and know exactly how much you drink.*

Have you reached a point where you are fully aware of your excessive drinking? Have you begun calculating the amount you drink each day? Are you constantly worried about how much you drink? Do you know the number of drinks in a bottle of wine versus a quart of hard liquor? Do you have a target number of drinks in mind for each day? Is that because you are trying to cut back?

*You keep trying to cut back.*

Do you promise yourself day after day that you will drink fewer drinks than you did the day before? Do you find that you still drink the same amount, anyway? Do you feel guilty when you go beyond what has been your normal heavy consumption of alcohol?

*You find excuses to stay home from work.*

Have you become creative in finding ways to work from home so you can drink? Have you ducked out from an assignment at work by using a flimsy reason to disappear early (and go home and drink)?

*You drink more than five drinks on a daily basis.*

Is drinking five or more drinks daily something that has been ongoing for several months or longer? Are you at the point where drinking does not give you a high until you have had at least four or five drinks? Is it a habit for you to drink more than five drinks whenever you can?

*You drink just as much, if not more, while on business travel.*

Do you stop at the store and stock up on booze while out of town on business? Do you buy just one bottle at a time and still go back to the store each day for more? Do you go out of your way to locate a liquor store in the area of your hotel? Do you drink in the hotel bar and then continue drinking in your hotel room?

*You drink so much that you have acquired a large gut.*

Has drinking become such an important habit that you ignore your gaining weight? Have you acquired a "beer gut?" Do you still wear pants that are too small for your growing waistline?

*You have blackouts.*

Often, after heavy drinking, an alcoholic may pass out and fall asleep. That sleep may equate to an alcohol blackout. When you wake up, do you remember little of what transpired before you slept? Do you recall only some of your previous activities prior to sleeping, but not specific details?
Equally dangerous are short blackouts, which may be brought on by chronic alcohol abuse. These blackouts may happen as a brief seizure, or mini seizure. You may not even realize when you have had a short blackout. You may lose consciousness briefly. You may experience blindness for a second or more. These types of blackouts can occur without warning with potentially disastrous results.

*My personal experience with blackouts*:

I could sometimes tell when I had experienced a mini blackout. I would suddenly find myself losing my balance and I would lose my sight for a split second or more. It could happen anywhere at anytime. I often worried about falling in the shower or blacking out while driving. It was particularly worrisome if I was driving with someone else in the car. I recall times when I would pull over and ask my passenger to drive because I feared I might have a blackout and cause an accident. I came to know when I was most susceptible. My blackouts were one of the main reasons I made the decision to get sober and remain sober. I knew it would be only a matter of time before I had a serious accident and I didn't want to be responsible for hurting someone else.

*You vomit blood.*

Have you ever vomited blood? This would likely indicate a very serious problem with a heavy drinker. It could mean there is internal bleeding, which is part of end-stage alcoholism. If you ever throw up blood, you should seek immediate medical attention. Such a condition is extremely urgent and has the potential to be fatal.

# Chapter 3: What To Do – Setting Your Mind to It

If you have purchased this book, you are already headed in the right direction. You have a desire to get sober again. That is your goal.

This is you now: You are in trouble. You are not physically well. You are physically addicted to alcohol and you may not even realize it. You could be in danger of dying from a seizure or an alcohol related illness or accident. As I have explained, you take a big risk by trying to stop cold turkey on your own. Once you have a physical addiction to alcohol, the only way to succeed in getting sober safely is to do it under proper medical supervision in a hospital. Yes, you need proper full-on inpatient care, and you will enjoy most of it.

Notice I said you are "headed" in the right direction? You are *already* taking action by reading this book. Keep that mindset and this simple plan will work for you. Your goal is to get sober and to stay sober so you can heal the damage done by alcohol. I won't even dictate to you how long you should remain sober. That is up to you, but even if you don't realize it now, you will realize, eventually, just how much you have missed while being pickled in alcohol.

Your life can become a whole lot more meaningful and enjoyable. You can feel productive again instead of just hanging-on until your next drink. Perhaps that is what you are doing at this very moment, right now. No one said you couldn't have a drink while you read this. When you get sober, you may never read this again, but *do* read this again if you need to. You could have a blackout after the first time you read this book, so you should keep it handy to read again to help you with your plan.

I said this was easy. It is. It is a simple matter of planning the time to get sober, just as if it were a vacation. The funny thing is it will feel like a vacation once you execute the plan. You just need to start by scheduling you plan.

Obtaining sobriety safely takes about one week. Set your mind to taking a week off from work and everything else in your life. It will be the best vacation you will ever have. You will be going into the hospital where they will take good care of you. You will be sleeping most of the time. Can it be any easier than that? You go in sick, you sleep for several days, and you come out fine. It's like being reborn. You may be a little groggy when you first leave the hospital, but your body will feel much better. You will come out of it feeling relaxed and comfortable in your own skin again.

So, set your mind to going ahead with this plan. Look at your calendar. Think about when you want to get this started. If it takes you another heavy binge to get further motivated, so be it. Set your mind to setting a start date. Mark it on a calendar and clear your schedule for that week.

Also, keep in mind that life happens. You may have to reschedule. This does not mean you need to cancel your plans to get sober. Remember, you need this. You can do this. Set your mind to setting aside a specific week for getting sober safely in a hospital.

Now think of all the reasons you have for getting sober. You have likely been thinking about this for a long time. Schedule a time and follow the simple plan provided in this book.

# Chapter 4: The New Tool
# Campral (Acamprosate) is Key

There is a new drug for treating alcohol dependency, which has just come on the market in recent years. It still surprises me how few people are aware of this significant advance in treating alcohol addiction. I found using the drug to be incredibly effective in helping me to stop drinking. The drug name is *Acamprosate*, more commonly known by its brand name, Campral.

Campral gave me my life back. *I* actually saved my *own* life by choosing to try this new drug therapy. Campral works in the brain to alleviate cravings for alcohol.

Here are a couple of source quotes describing Campral:

<u>U.S. National Library of Medicine</u>
<u>National Institutes of Health</u>
<u>National Center for Biotechnology Information U.S. National Library of Medicine National Institutes of Health</u>:

"Acamprosate (a kam' pro sate)

Why is this medication prescribed?
Acamprosate is used along with counseling and social support to help people who have stopped drinking large amounts of alcohol (alcoholism) to avoid drinking alcohol again. Drinking alcohol for a long time changes the way the brain works. Acamprosate works by helping the brains of people who have drunk large amounts of alcohol to work normally again. Acamprosate does not prevent the withdrawal symptoms that people may

experience when they stop drinking alcohol. Acamprosate has not been shown to work in people who have not stopped drinking alcohol or in people who drink large amounts of alcohol and also overuse or abuse other substances such as street drugs or prescription medications."

Food and Drug Administration (FDA) of the United States:

The FDA approved this drug (Acamprosate) in July 2004, releasing this statement:

"While its mechanism of action is not fully understood, Campral is thought to act on the brain pathways related to alcohol abuse. Campral was demonstrated to be safe and effective by multiple placebo-controlled clinical studies involving alcohol-dependent patients who had already been withdrawn from alcohol, (i.e., detoxified). Campral proved superior to placebo in maintaining abstinence (keeping patients off alcohol consumption), as indicated by a greater percentage of acamprosate-treated subjects being assessed as continuously abstinent throughout treatment. Campral is not addicting. In clinical trials, it was well tolerated. The most common adverse events reported for patients taking Campral included headache, diarrhea, flatulence, and nausea."

Acamprosate helps to prevent you from drinking alcohol only as long as you are taking it. It is recommended that you continue taking acamprosate even if you do not think you are likely to start drinking alcohol again. Do not stop taking acamprosate without talking to your doctor.

If you drink alcohol while you are taking acamprosate, you should continue to take the medication and call your doctor. Acamprosate will not cause you to have any unpleasant drug reaction if you drink alcohol during treatment.

I experienced no side effects at all while on Campral therapy. Your doctor should consider any possible interactions with other medications you may already be taking. The term *therapy* is used here strictly in the sense of taking Campral as a therapeutic drug regimen. My use of the term, "therapy" only relates to the taking of Campral. It has nothing to do with psychological counseling or any other cognitive therapies.

In the simplest terms, based on my experience, Campral therapy changed my mindset significantly for the better. The following chapter explains.

# Chapter 5: This is Remarkable!
# Daily Living and Campral Therapy

Here are some important and encouraging things to know about Campral: This drug is not a mood-altering drug. It is not a controlled substance. I did not experience any significant change in my normal, everyday mood, at any time, over the course of the year in which I took Campral. The most pronounced and noticeable change I experienced was simply a complete loss of craving for alcohol. This was possible for me only after first detoxifying in the hospital for a week. Campral would not have helped me through a withdrawal on my own. I would still likely have had seizures and other severe withdrawal symptoms from alcohol, even while taking Campral. Remember, you need to detoxify safely under medical supervision *first* before beginning Campral drug therapy.

There is no chemical dependency with use of Campral. There is no toxic interaction if you drink while on Campral therapy. However, common sense says that drinking while taking Campral is obviously counterproductive. In the event of a slip or relapse, Campral therapy may still be continued. It is highly recommended that you consult your doctor if you relapse. Depending on the amount of alcohol consumed during the relapse, you may need medical attention again to manage possible alcohol withdrawal symptoms.

The most remarkable thing about Campral, for me, was my loss of craving for alcohol. It was nearly absolute. I speak solely from my own experience. Once I was out of the hospital and taking the drug, I soon realized my mind wasn't preoccupied with getting something alcoholic to drink. I would think about alcohol only within the context of how utterly amazed I was that I could push thoughts of drinking from my mind easily, and how strange it was that those thoughts would not keep coming back. I could visit the grocery store and walk past the alcohol aisle, ignoring the bottles of wine and vodka. I kept waiting for some involuntary urge to cause me to wander over to the booze section, but it did not happen. I would think about drinking occasionally, particularly around dinnertime, the time when I usually had a glass of wine or two (or ten) with dinner, yet I was able to move on and change my way of thinking over time. It never became a difficult struggle for me.

I did not attend any group counseling or individual psychological therapy while on my new course of abstinence from alcohol. Having tried those methods in the past, I had long ago concluded they were not effective for me. In fact, I realized that when I had participated in those programs they had only made me feel worse about myself. I had always felt a need to get away from the negativity. I never found it productive to listen to other people's woes and failures while trying to tackle my own problems. Some people may enjoy the sense of belonging by going to group meetings, however I never wanted to become comfortable telling sad stories and listening to other people's gripes for hours on end in my spare time. I very rarely found anything useful or uplifting about those sessions—rather, just the opposite.

Taking Campral, I realized that after about six months my brain chemistry seemed normal again. I say, "seemed normal," because I have no written, documented, scientific explanation of exactly what happened inside my brain. I just know that I found myself safely living without alcohol. I easily became accustomed to living without it. Campral had somehow adjusted my brain chemistry to stop craving alcohol.

Now, I can even go to restaurants and not even think of ordering a pre-dinner cocktail or a glass of wine with dinner. I recall avoiding restaurants in my first weeks after obtaining sobriety, but I soon found I was entirely in control of my actions. I had no need or craving for a drink. I was able to change an old habit without breaking out in a sweat over it.

After a year, I gradually reduced my dose of Campral. It is always safer to taper off with any drug therapy than to stop all at once. Again, there is no dependency with Campral, so there were really no concerns about withdrawal. I just chose to taper off for my own peace of mind. Perhaps it was just me proving to myself that I could do it on my own terms. At this writing, I am in my fourth year of complete sobriety without a single "slip." It has not been difficult. I have not had to go to any miserable meetings full of sad stories to achieve this. I feel good about myself and I have accomplished far more than I had expected in these last few years of being sober.

# Chapter 6: My Plan — Your Plan

Follow these steps for safely obtaining sobriety. Each action listed below includes additional background information to make it easy to understand and to execute:

1. See your doctor and ask for a prescription for Campral. Explain that you need it to help you in your goal to stop drinking. Your doctor will understand. *You should have no problem getting a prescription since Campral is not a controlled substance and there are no dependency issues whatsoever.

2. Check with local hospitals to find out the easiest way to gain admission for detoxification. This process may differ from hospital to hospital. Many hospitals will admit a walk-in patient through the emergency room check-in for detoxification. Explain you are dependent on alcohol and have stopped drinking. Trained medical professionals know that detoxification is a critical procedure that requires inpatient care. Explain (if necessary) that you have strong concerns about withdrawal and cannot do it safely at home. *Do not become discouraged or daunted by this step.* (Alcohol withdrawal *is* a serious medical condition that requires supervised treatment.) While in the hospital, the process will involve you being administered intravenous fluids,

anti-seizure drugs, as well as sleep inducement drugs during detoxification and withdrawal. Your hospital stay may last three days to a week, or more. The only way to proceed effectively with Campral therapy is after a thorough detoxification.

3. Begin taking Campral immediately upon release from the hospital. Rest at home for a few more days, if needed, while any sedation drugs wear off. The hospital will reduce the doses of sleep medications toward the end of your stay. (Depending on your situation and medical history, you may also be prescribed anti-seizure drugs. Be sure to take those, if prescribed.)

4. Once you have become alert and active, be aware of yourself and your thoughts about alcohol and drinking. Try not to dwell on the idea of having a drink, but allow yourself to marvel at how easy it is to push away thoughts of drinking. You will find you can easily change your course.

\*In my case, three years ago, my doctor was unfamiliar with the new drug, Campral. She took a few minutes to look it up, and then wrote a prescription for me without hesitation. As of this writing, Campral should be more widely known by now. It is already widely available.

## Chapter 7: Remind Yourself of Pending Disaster

If you are drinking heavily now and have serious concerns about your survival, you need to ask yourself, how long do you think you can survive? Disaster is just around the corner as long as you continue living in an alcohol-induced fog. I can say this because disaster has happened to me. I needed to be hospitalized three times. I could have died any number of times.

Here are just a couple of the things that could happen if you continue to ignore your dire situation: You could black out at the wheel of your car while driving and have a terrible accident that could end your life as well as the lives of others. You could suffer a fall in the shower and seriously injure yourself. A bad hit on the head could render you incapacitated and make you dependent upon others indefinitely. Those are just examples. There are plenty of other, less obvious means, by which alcohol can do you in. What will you choose as your legacy?

At some point, you could eventually reach the final stages of alcoholism (liver disease and stomach ulcers). Perhaps then, you would try to stop drinking on your own. Or, you might simply find yourself in a situation where there is no alcohol available and you are unable to obtain alcohol. In either case, you could suffer seizures from withdrawal if you stopped drinking suddenly. Your loved ones could be traumatized at the sight of your body in spasms, shaking, and with seizures of rigidity as your eyes rolled back in your head. You would be a frightening spectacle while having a gran mal seizure. Your breathing may even stop and you could die without immediate emergency medical attention. You could die alone or right in front of those who love you as your body shuts down from a malfunction brought on by years of toxic alcohol.

This may sound harsh, but I find I can call on these thoughts to help me stay sober when, say, after so many years of not drinking, I occasionally entertain the thought of having a drink. I don't wish to start that cycle all over again. I went through hell to stop, finally. I remind myself of that sometimes. I rarely need to, but I do remember my own disasters.

# Chapter 8: Conclusion

You are not alone. There is help all around you. I have pulled together the most important pieces and put them into a simple plan. It can be incredibly difficult to achieve a goal if you don't have all of the tools you need—if you don't even know what's out there. Fortunately, you do not have to make a spectacle of yourself, or die trying, in order to obtain sobriety safely. You can do it with dignity once you have a plan. That is why I wrote this book. I thought it would help others in the same situation. A few years ago, when I was in over my head and when I had finally realized what I really needed, I was able to put my mind to it and come up with a plan to get sober. It is not that complicated. There are only a few steps, but they are the right ones. My plan worked for me and I know it can work for you. This is for the person who just can't seem to stop drinking.

I know there are persons out there who are now in an ongoing struggle. Nobody told me what actions to take to get out of my seemingly impossible situation. When I came to realize that I was not only mentally addicted to alcohol, but physically addicted too, I knew I needed some serious help. I was having seizures whenever I tried to stop drinking! Most people have not been through as much as I have as relates to alcohol abuse and the treatment odyssey. Most people do not know about their options. I discovered some new options after I had already tried the old ones. I weighed them all and put them together in my simple plan, which I was able to follow myself, successfully.

Once I became sober again, it was suggested to me that I write this book. Friends and family encouraged me to write about what I had done. They had listened when I told them I had formulated a simple plan to get sober. They watched as I eventually made the time and implemented it. They were glad when I completed my plan successfully. It took awhile for some people to realize I was actually sober again, and was staying sober. I did not need to go through another long rehab program. I simply decided to stay sober once I had safely obtained sobriety again.

    I believe I got it right this time. I hope this plan works for you too.

    Best regards and good luck!

    George Legacy

www.ingramcontent.com/pod-product-compliance
Lightning Source LLC
Chambersburg PA
CBHW061259040426
42444CB00010B/2420